FARMS OLD AND NEW

LIFE ON THE FARM

Lynn M. Stone

Rourke Publishing LLC
Vero Beach, Florida 32964

12885539

www.rourkepublishing.com

PHOTO CREDITS:
All photos © Lynn M. Stone

EDITORIAL SERVICES:
Pamela Schroeder

Library of Congress Cataloging-in-Publication Data

Stone, Lynn M.
    Farms old and new / Lynn M. Stone
        p. cm. — (Life on the farm)
    Includes bibliographical references (p.).
    ISBN 1-58952-094-7
        1. Family farms—United States—Juvenile literature. [1. Farms.] I. Title.

S519 .S76 2001
630'.973—dc21   2001031678

Printed in the USA

TABLE OF CONTENTS

Farms Old and New   5

Old Farms   9

Changing Farms   16

New Farms   20

Glossary   23

Index   24

Further Reading/Websites to Visit   24

FARMS OLD AND NEW

There are nearly 2 million farms in the United States. They are important to everyone. They produce most of the food we eat. Fruit, vegetables, meat, and dairy **products** come from farms.

Farmers produce food in fields, orchards, groves, and barns.

America's favorite farms are the small family farms that raise **livestock**. But these farms are disappearing. There are fewer this year than last. There will be even fewer next year. Old, broken barns stand empty in many parts of the United States.

All farms will not disappear. After all, everyone needs to eat! But farms and farming have changed.

Small family-owned dairy farms like this have been disappearing in America at a fast rate.

OLD FARMS

In America during the 1700s, most families lived on small farms. People farmed because they wanted to eat. Families could not always plan on having deer or wild turkeys on the table. Farming was a much safer bet than hunting. Farming could be done at home, too.

Most Americans used to live on small farms with wooden fences and buildings.

9

In the 1700s farm work was very hard. A farmer could raise enough food for his family, but not much more than that. There were few farm machines of any kind. None of them had engines. The farmer, with his horses, mules, and **oxen**, did the work.

The farm family raised its own animals, mostly chickens, pigs, and cattle. The farmer planted corn and garden vegetables. The family had a few fruit trees. They raised hay and sometimes some wheat.

Farmers used to tend their fields with the strength of their backs and their horses.

Early settlers used Devon cattle like this for meat, milk, and work. Modern breeds of cattle are used for one purpose only.

Most hogs are raised indoors.

The farm family **butchered** its own animals. They made their own butter. They cured their meat and canned vegetables. Most of the family's clothes were homemade.

The American farms of the 1700s and well into the 1800s were like little malls. Whatever you needed was there. But you had to work hard to get it.

Farm women used to make their own wool yarn on wooden looms.

CHANGING FARMS

In the second half of the 1800s, new machines were invented. They were powered by steam, then gasoline. Machines changed America.

Machines could be used to make all kinds of things. Factories were built. Cities grew with workers for the factories. City people needed farm products. With machines, farm work could be done faster and better. Now farmers could grow more than they needed for their families. With new railroads, farmers could send their products to the city.

The tractor and other farm machines changed the way people farmed in North America.

American farmers began to grow just one or two crops. They became better at raising crops and animals. By 1900, only about half of Americans lived on farms. Today fewer than three of every 100 Americans live on farms.

Modern farms specialize by raising just one or two products. This is a New York dairy farm, which raises milking cows.

NEW FARMS

Modern American farms produce huge amounts of food. Science has helped. Scientists have made new types of food plants and **improved** animal **breeds**. New fertilizers help crop plants, like corn, grow bigger and faster. Modern farms grow more food with less land—and fewer full-time farmers. American farms feed Americans and many people around the world. The United States **exports** more food than any other country.

Improved breed Holstein cows give much more milk than Holsteins of the past.

Modern American farms have changed. Many are owned by **companies**, not families. Many farm animals are raised indoors. Growing cities have moved into what used to be farm country. Farmlands are sold to make way for homes and highways.

Farms will always be here. But fewer and fewer of them will be the small, family-run farms of the past.

GLOSSARY

breed (BREED) — within a kind of domestic animal, one special type, such as *Holstein* cattle

butchered (BOOCH erd) — to turn animals into food

company (KUM pch nee) — a business run by a group of people to make money

exports (EK sports) — those products that are made in one country and shipped to another

improved (im PROOVD) — made better

livestock (LYV stahk) — farm animals

oxen (AHK sen) — male cattle tamed and used to pull heavy loads

product (PRAHD ekt) — that which is made or produced

INDEX

animals   11, 14, 19, 22
barns   6
clothes   14
crops   19
dairy products   5
families   9, 11, 14, 16, 22

farm work   11, 16
food   5, 20
livestock   6
machines   11, 16
meat   5, 14
vegetables   5, 11, 14

Further Reading

Halley, Ned. *Eyewitness: Farm*. Dorling Kindersley, 2000.
Kalman, Bobbie. *In the Barn.* Crabtree, 2000.
Splear, Elsie Lww. *Growing Seasons*. Penguin Putnam, 2000.

Websites To Visit

www.alhfam.org
www.osv.org

About The Author

Lynn Stone is the author of more than 400 children's books. He is a talented natural history photographer as well. Lynn, a former teacher, travels worldwide to photograph wildlife in its natural habitat.